Be
Mindful
and
Simplify
Your Life

KATE JAMES

Andrews McMeel
PUBLISHING®

Praise for Kate James and Total Balance

"I absolutely adore Kate. She is a highly skilled, generous, and enormously gifted business coach, especially for those who don't traditionally consider themselves 'business people.'"
— *Clare Bowditch, Big Hearted Business*

"Kate really 'walks the talk' and is clearly someone who has a great deal of expertise to share. Thank you, Kate!"
— *Robert Gerrish, Flying Solo*

"Kate James is a generous, creative coach who is passionate about helping others fulfill their dreams and brilliant at helping people move through both inner and outer obstacles."
— *Elise Bialylew, Founder of Mindful in May*

"I would not hesitate to recommend Kate James of Total Balance to anyone who has goals and dreams, be it for life or business, that they want to achieve and don't know where to begin, or how to get there."
— *Jodie Holmes, Director of Seaside Creative*

"Put simply, working with Kate helped me to get clear—which has been nothing short of life changing."
— *Leanne Clancey, Food & Travel Writer*

Contents

Introduction

Mindfulness is about being aware, being accepting, and being kind to yourself and others as you navigate your way through life. You could say that living mindfully is learning to value "being" as much as you value "doing."

In the work I have done with clients over the past eighteen years, I've observed that the happiest people usually keep things simple. They know how to enjoy the present, they spend time reflecting on their choices, and they are proactive about making changes in their lives. They do all of these things in a mindful way. They accept that life won't always be easy, and they're willing to roll with the punches when things don't go to plan. Crucially, they live on their own terms, without being overly caught up in what everyone else is doing.

These people are proof that one of the greatest ways to encourage happiness is to fully embrace mindfulness.

The basic principles of mindfulness include:

> Awareness (of your senses, breath, your body, your
> environment, your thoughts, and your physical experience).

> Being non-judgmental (allowing things to be as they are).

> Practicing compassion and acceptance (learning to be
> considerate of ourselves and others).

> Savoring the moment (not worrying about what happened
> before or what might happen next).

Within this little book, I'll introduce my version of what it means
to live mindfully. I'll provide you with practical tips on how being
mindful can lead to a less complicated and more fulfilling life.

Explore the book in your own way. Read it from front to back
if you feel so inclined, or open it at a section that draws your
attention. You'll find that certain aspects of mindfulness appeal
to you more than others, and you'll know intuitively which areas
need to be addressed first. The most important thing is to be
open to the idea of being mindful in all areas of your life. The
very fact that you're reading this is a good start: you've set the
intention, so you are already on your way.

1. What is mindful living?

Understanding mindfulness is only a starting point—to live mindfully, you must take the basic principles outlined in the Introduction and apply them every day. This means:

> Making contact with the present moment.

> Being aware of your thoughts and feelings.

> Being mindful of your behaviors and actions.

> Taking a mindful approach to longer-term planning.

> Making a mindful contribution to something bigger than yourself.

In many ways, we can use the word "mindfulness" interchangeably with "awareness." Living a more mindful life means paying attention to the choices we make, rather than operating on autopilot.

WHEN WE BEGIN TO DO THIS, WE GAIN CLARITY ABOUT WHAT REALLY MATTERS AND WE STRIP AWAY SOME OF THE COMPLEXITY OF LIFE.

Initially, you may find that introducing new ideas feels less simple, but in the long run, you'll recognize that mindful living means being more aligned with your personal values and ultimately discovering a way of life where you're more at peace with things as they are.

2. Are you living mindfully?

How mindful are you? Give yourself one point for every "yes," half a point for a "maybe," and zero for every "no."

I'm aware, at least some of the time, of being in the moment.

———————————

I am aware of my thoughts much of the time.

———————————

I make an effort to be compassionate with myself and others.

———————————

I'm okay with not being perfect.

———————————

I accept that I can't control life, and I know how to let go when things don't go my way.

———————————

I'm okay with having difficult feelings sometimes.

———————————

When something good is happening in my life, I take time to appreciate it before moving on to the next thing.

———————————

I notice changes in my body when my emotions change, like my heart racing or my muscles tensing if I feel stressed.

I occasionally spend time alone to take stock of what's important.

When I'm walking outside, I'm aware of my surroundings.

I know how to fully experience my senses.

I listen to my intuition.

When I eat, I really taste my food, and I only eat until I'm full.

I am a good listener.

I'm able to take care of myself as well as I take care of others.

I know how to forgive myself and other people when things have gone wrong.

I feel confident about the way I manage the practical aspects of my life, such as my career, my finances, and my living environment.

I am able to balance enjoying the "here and now" with mindfully planning for the future.

Are you living mindfully?

I'm able to accept that life
will be a mix of challenges
and happy experiences.

I make conscious choices
about how I treat the
environment.

/20

If you scored 15 or over, you're more mindful than most
people. Read through the tips, and maybe consider gifting this
book to a friend who needs it more.

Anywhere between 10 and 15, you're doing okay, but you could
do with some positive change. Flip through the book for ideas.

If you scored 10 or below, you might benefit from some support
from a mindfulness coach or psychologist, as well as trying the
tips included here.

THE MOST IMPORTANT THING
IS GETTING STARTED, SO MAKE
SURE YOU COMPLETE ONE
ACTION STEP THIS WEEK.

3. The opposite of living mindfully

The opposite of mindfulness—and the way we are all prone to think particularly during challenging times—is mindlessness.

Have you ever walked into a room and forgotten why you went there? Forgotten to turn the car headlights on (or forgotten to turn them off)? Do you feel like you're usually reacting to things rather than working on a plan? How many times have you found yourself distracted while in conversation?

These days, there are so many demands on our time and so much information overload that it's increasingly challenging to stay centered, calm, and focused.

Instead, we may feel anxious, vague, or off-balance—like we're always catching up, or like the proverbial hamster in a wheel. And that's no way to live.

The opposite of living mindfully

The only way to break that cycle is to *consciously choose* to live more mindfully, and one of the simple ways to begin to do this is to observe yourself throughout your day.

Try this

Set a reminder in your calendar or an alarm on your phone to ring every two hours for the next couple of days.

When the alarm goes off, check in and observe yourself as though from a distance. Check your posture, your stress levels, and your mood. Are you being mindful or mindless in your approach to your day and the people around you?

You might find a few tips in this book that will make a big difference to your sense of well-being, and you may find that it's actually pretty simple to start changing your life for the better.

IT'S IMPORTANT THAT YOU DON'T
SEE THIS AS AN OPPORTUNITY
TO BEAT YOURSELF UP. INSTEAD,
THINK OF IT AS A CHANCE TO BE
AWARE, SO THAT YOU CAN SEE
WHERE YOU NEED CHANGE MOST.

4. Be present and withhold judgment

There are two main reasons most of us feel stressed: we spend too little time living in the present moment and too much energy wanting to change it. In order to cultivate inner peace, we need to work on these elements. These are two of the basic principles of mindfulness.

1. BE PRESENT

Bring your attention to what you're doing right now. You might try this while you're reading. As you do, you'll probably notice that your mind naturally wants to wander away from the content of the book. Momentarily stop what you're doing and say to yourself, "I'm reading." Then bring your attention back with a greater sense of awareness.

Be present and withhold judgment

Next, try it with the routines of everyday life. Say to yourself, "I'm driving my car." "I'm walking up stairs." "I'm washing the dishes." "I'm listening to my partner." "I'm writing an email."

It's unlikely that you'll be able to be fully present for long stretches of time initially, but practicing for a few minutes every day slowly builds a new awareness that makes it easier to stay in the moment.

2. WITHHOLD JUDGMENT

Once you are present to an experience, become aware of the thoughts accompanying that experience. It's likely that you'll notice judgments such as: "The traffic is terrible." "I'm tired." "I can't stand this." "My partner is annoying me." "I'm bored."

As best you can, withhold any judgment for a moment or two and see how it changes the way that you feel. Forgive the situation if you need to—allow it to just be.

You'll discover a great sense of calm when you can learn to be with things as they are. Later in the book, we'll explore how to make change mindfully when it's required.

5. You are not your mind

Fifteen years ago, Eckhart Tolle wrote a book called The Power of Now, *which quickly became a bestseller. Eckhart describes how he transformed his own life, going from "despair to self-realization" by learning to take control of his thoughts.*

The basic premise of his book is that "you are not your mind." If you can learn to become the observer of your thoughts rather than being overtaken by them, you'll spend less time struggling with life.

Create a silent observer

Imagine a version of yourself who can be the silent observer of the chatter inside your mind. You might find it easier to think that this "silent observer" sits outside of you. Their role is to watch what goes on inside your mind.

You are not your mind

This might not feel easy at first but persist for a bit so that you learn about the behavior of your mind. It's likely that you'll notice lots of judgments about yourself, about others, and about how things *should* be. Do your best to label your thoughts, "judging," "criticizing," "planning," "worrying," etc. and allow them to just be there for now.

Don't try to change your thoughts, but rather notice and name the thoughts that are here.

6. Mindful meditation

Meditation and mindfulness are not exactly the same thing. Mindfulness describes the state of being, *while meditation is the* practice *where you either sit or move in a mindful way to increase your awareness and to help to quiet your mind.*

In order to cultivate a more mindful approach to life, ideally, you would meditate every day. Even five minutes will give you a boost; what's most important is that you make time to meditate on a regular basis so that it starts to become an essential element in your life.

Many people let their meditation practice go too quickly because they think they're not doing it right, but here's something important you need to know before you begin:

THERE'S NO WRONG WAY TO MEDITATE. JUST MAKE THE TIME— THAT'S ALL THAT MATTERS.

It's normal for your mind to wander during meditation, and you may well experience boredom or restlessness. If you can learn to be with these feelings, you will lay down a foundation for accepting the challenges you encounter in everyday life.

Try it for yourself

Find a quiet place where you won't be interrupted and take a seat in a comfy chair. Close your eyes and bring your awareness to your breath. It's likely that as you try to focus on the breath, you'll notice how busy your mind is. This is completely normal. Allow your thoughts to be there and then bring your attention back to your breathing. You might find that it helps to picture your mind as a sky and the random thoughts as clouds that you gently blow away when you exhale.

Imagine you can follow the path of the breath from outside the body and, as you do, pay close attention to all of the aspects of your breathing. Notice the sound of the breath, the temperature of the breath, the rise and fall of your abdomen, the movement in your belly as your lungs fill with air. Follow all of these sensations as the breath leaves your body too.

If you're comfortable to continue with a focus on your breathing, use the breath as your "object of focus" throughout the rest of your meditation. If this feels uncomfortable in any way, try using a mantra instead: repeat a word or phrase silently under your breath for the duration of your meditation. Use the word "release" or, if you prefer, a more traditional Sanskrit mantra—try "om" or "so hum." You don't need to say the words out loud, just repeat them silently. Think of the sound as an anchor to help focus the attention in the mind.

Continue to practice for as long as you feel comfortable, or set an alarm that uses a gentle tone such as a chime. You'll find a range of free meditation timer apps online that can help with this.

At the end of your meditation, open your eyes and take in your surroundings. Take the time to bring your perspective back from your meditation into your real life and feel the positive

Mindful meditation

influence it will have. You might even like to visualize your day and how you'll approach it.

It can take some time to fully experience the benefits of meditation, so if you're not noticing any immediate change, don't give up yet. It's worth sticking with it for at least a few weeks.

You'll know that it's working when you find yourself in situations where you don't react the way you'd normally react.

FOR EXAMPLE, WHEN SOMETHING HAPPENS THAT WOULD NORMALLY STRESS YOU OUT, INSTEAD OF GETTING AGITATED, YOU'LL DISCOVER THAT YOU'RE ABLE TO TAP INTO AN INNER WELL OF CALM. IT'S AN ABSOLUTE REVELATION.

We often sit still to meditate,
but we can be mindful anywhere.

———

You can't meditate unless
you are being mindful.

———

Use an "object of focus" to
quiet your mind. Choose
either breath or a mantra.

———

You don't need to empty
your mind to meditate.

———

It's normal to have thoughts.

———

There's no wrong way to meditate.

How to meditate when you can't sit still

If the idea of sitting still to meditate isn't your cup of tea, there are other ways to enjoy a meditative state that will help you feel a greater sense of calm and lead you to be more mindful.

Any experience that allows you to focus on one thing to the exclusion of all else, temporarily emptying your mind of all the clutter of your thoughts, can be considered a meditation.

Listening to certain styles of music can be meditative, and many forms of physical activity take us into a meditative mindset. Dancing, running and swimming, and doing yoga, Tai Chi, or surfing can be meditations in themselves.

The key to making your physical experience more "mindful" is to focus on key elements, tuning into very specific things. Focus on your body, your breathing, the rhythm of your movement, and the sounds you can hear. Tune in to everything around you without judgment. The focus itself is a meditation.

7. Find happiness within

Most of us imagine that once we find the perfect partner, reach our ideal weight, land our dream job, or move to the right city, then *we'll feel completely fulfilled.*

In 2012, psychologists and happiness experts Kennon Sheldon and Sonja Lyubomirsky wrote a paper about "hedonic adaptation," a term that describes our ability to quickly adapt to positive change. They found that while we might be happier for a little while if we win the lottery or fall in love, within a short space of time, our happiness levels return to what they were.

TRUE HAPPINESS RESIDES WITHIN.
IT'S NOT SOMETHING WE WILL
FIND LOOKING OUTSIDE.

How to be happier now

> Make peace with some of your personal flaws and give yourself permission to be imperfect.

> Make room for imperfection in others too.

> Let go of unrealistic expectations of how your life should be.

> Stop telling yourself you'll be happy once your life is different. Appreciate and feel grateful for things that are good in your life right now.

> Keep your life interesting by continuing to try new things. This has been proven to be one of the factors that lead to lasting happiness.

8. One thing at a time

It's difficult to multitask in a mindful way, primarily because being mindful means being focused, and we can only really focus on one thing at a time.

We might joke about women being great at multitasking, but, according to ADAA (Anxiety and Depression Association of America), women are also twice as likely as men to have an anxiety disorder. Maybe all of this multitasking isn't helping!

Often we do two things at once to avoid boredom. When we create a habit of having lots of stimulation, we lose the ability to block out distractions and focus on one task at a time. We also run the risk of never being present to anything we are doing, and the longer-term consequence is that we can find it difficult to slow down and relax.

One thing at a time

Research conducted by Stanford University tells us that multitasking actually makes us less productive. Try being aware of when you habitually take on more than one activity at a time, and practice being more focused.

Multitasking you should be mindful to avoid

> Reading emails while talking on the phone.

> Eating while watching television or using a device.

> Using devices in meetings.

> Reading, emailing, or looking at social media when your partner, your children, or your friend is speaking to you about something important (or talking to you about anything at all, really).

If you must multitask

There are times when you may find it necessary to multitask, such as when you're genuinely short on time. If you must do two things at once, do them with the awareness that you're multitasking.

9. Be aware of the "busy" trap

Most of us feel stressed because we're rushing from one thing to the next, and we're too busy to enjoy life. Some of this busyness is unavoidable, but some of it is self-imposed.

We usually over-commit when we fear missing out, when we want to please other people, or when we want to appear to the outside world to be living interesting, exciting lives.

All of us need a small amount of downtime every day—even if it's only fifteen or twenty minutes—and ideally, we should have at least half a day of rest every week.

Being mindful of the "busy" trap

> Over the next week or so, start to think about how you currently fill your days. You'll become aware that there are some tasks that are "non-negotiable." For example, going to work, preparing meals, sleeping, taking care of children or elderly parents, and personal admin tasks.

> Consider whether you're making time for activities that support your well-being. These might include exercise, meditation, time alone, time pursuing activities that energize you, and social activities you enjoy.

> Next, think about the things that you do because you think you should be doing them or because other people expect you to do them. Look at the activities that don't add value to your life, such as watching trashy television, spending lots of time on social media, or surfing the internet mindlessly.

> Review all of the activities you include in a standard week. Are you trying to do too much? Are you doing enough for your well-being? Is there anything you can let go of or turn down? Are you realistic in the expectations you place upon yourself? What can you change in order to make your life less busy?

EVEN SMALL CHANGES MAKE A DIFFERENCE. FOR EXAMPLE, IN YOUR WORKDAY, BLOCK OUT THIRTY MINUTES TO GET AWAY FROM YOUR USUAL WORKSPACE TO EAT LUNCH OR GO FOR A WALK. SWITCH OFF YOUR EMAIL AT A SET TIME EACH NIGHT. KEEP AT LEAST A FEW HOURS OF EACH WEEKEND FREE.

10. Savor the good

We know that our minds have a strong bias toward negative thoughts and that painful experiences are more memorable than positive ones.

Rick Hanson is a neuropsychologist who says we can balance this negative bias by learning to "take in the good." Instead of letting positive experiences slip by without us noticing them, we need to actively seek them out, really enjoy them and let them sink into our psyche. If we do this often enough, we will create new neural pathways in our brains, making it easier for us to feel more positive in the long-term.

Try this

1. Several times throughout your day, make a point of noticing something positive. It might be enjoying your morning coffee, completing a task well, or spending time with someone you like. They don't need to be big things. Notice any tendency to dismiss the exercise as silly or vain (particularly when it comes to noticing the good in yourself).

---

2. Stay with the positive experience for, say, thirty seconds, and really let it fill your mind. Experience it with as many senses as possible—be fully aware of all of the aspects that are good. Holding a positive thought in your awareness literally helps to create new connections in your brain, but you need to work at it.

---

3. Imagine that the "good" is sinking right into you. Over time, these positive experiences add up, and they ultimately improve your mood, lower your stress levels, and help you to build a more resilient approach to life.

---

11. Seek joy

One of the first things we lose when we're busy and stressed is the childlike sense of wonder that allows us to experience life as a gift rather than something to be endured.

Being mindful doesn't mean always being serious. It's equally about being willing to open up to joyous, lighthearted experiences. Like all of the activities that will encourage you to live more mindfully, seeking joy requires a dedicated, intentional approach.

Give yourself permission to believe in the power of joy.

Rediscover joy

Dance in your kitchen.

Play the ukulele.

Play with the kids on their level.

Sing with your headphones in.

Fly a kite.

Draw a picture or make something creative.

Visit a gallery.

Be frivolous!

Seek out a festival of some sort.

Go to the movies during the day.

Take up a new hobby.

Give each of your senses a treat.

12. Slow it down

How many times have you rushed into things without planning them properly first (and had regrets afterward)? The instinct to launch into activities and get them done as quickly as possible may feel natural, but it is not always the best way to operate.

Thinking about what you want to do first, planning it, and being methodical: that's a mindful approach. It also makes the "doing" more enjoyable because you're working on a plan and aware of your progress rather than mindlessly rushing to complete a task.

When we do things in haste, we often make mistakes and create longer-term problems. Rushing makes us anxious and increases our stress hormones, which in time impacts our immune system and can ultimately make us physically unwell. When we're busy and stressed, we're also less inclined to enjoy the simple pleasures of life.

Being speedy also has an impact on the people around you. You know what it's like to be in the company of someone who's high strung—they're not someone you enjoy being with for long periods of time. You probably know what it's like to be in your own whirlwind of madness from time to time, and you don't want to be swept up in another person's.

Be aware of signs that you might be overdoing it yourself, like when you're waiting impatiently for the kettle to boil or are rushing into a yoga class or something else that is supposed to make you feel relaxed. Watch your internal language too. If phrases such as "I'll just quickly get this done," or "I'll just run and do that," pop into your head, it might be time to take a breather.

YOU CAN DO THINGS EFFICIENTLY WITHOUT DOING THEM IN A STRESSED OR PANICKY WAY. START BY CONSCIOUSLY SLOWING DOWN.

Slow it down

Check your speed

Identify your current "rev level." Are you running at a comfortable 5 out of 10, or do you feel as though you're "revving" at up around 8 or 9 out of 10? Catch yourself throughout the day and ask, "What speed am I doing now?" If you're going at 8 or 9 for sustained periods, be aware that you're probably being a bit reckless and are liable to crash or burn out.

Keep an eye on the activities, people, or situations that cause you to speed up.

> Slow down your conversations.

> Walk at a more leisurely pace.

> Take your time eating a meal.

> When you make yourself a cup of tea or get a glass of water, do it slowly and mindfully.

> Do one thing at a time.

- Arrive at appointments five minutes early.

- Write an important email and save it as a draft so that you can review it again before sending.

- Tell someone you'll get back to them before automatically saying "yes" to an extra commitment.

- Walk away from a conversation when you feel yourself getting frustrated, and revisit it when you feel calmer.

- If you're going through a stressful period, try a more gentle form of exercise like yoga or Pilates.

- Keep an eye on your language and avoid using phrases that make you feel like you need to rush. You might even mentally replace "I'll just quickly get this done," with "I've got time to do this properly."

- Make time to reconnect with your instincts.

13. Be grounded

Being grounded means, basically, being connected to what's real (as opposed to spinning out over what's happening in your head). It is about bringing your awareness back to your body so that you can be more emotionally and physically present. Your mind will wander less to the future or the past while you enjoy the here and now. Being grounded will help you to feel more balanced and in greater control of what you're thinking and doing.

As well as making you feel more present and aware, being grounded helps you feel centered and focused when you're communicating, which makes it particularly useful during difficult conversations. It also increases your confidence when you're making decisions or speaking in front of groups, and it helps calm your nerves in situations that might otherwise cause anxiety.

How to feel grounded

Stand up and feel your feet making physical contact with the floor. Imagine you feel a strong connection with the energy of the earth. Better still, plant your bare feet in a grassy lawn or in sand on a beach (even visualizing this will help). Imagine you have a sense of the earth's natural energy coming up through the soles of your feet.

If, after a minute or two, you're still not feeling grounded, try this creative trick. Envision breathing in a bright light that's coming down from above you, and imagine that the light travels right through your body, connecting deeply into the earth.

When you start feeling distracted, or you notice your attention has wandered away from your body, gently bring the awareness back without trying to force it. Practice being grounded a couple of times each day until it feels like something you can do naturally and easily.

14. Practice gratitude

Gratitude is an expression of appreciation for the goodness in life. If you're feeling grateful, you're being mindful, because you can't feel gratitude without first bringing your attention to what you're experiencing.

Positive psychology researchers tell us that practicing gratitude has a significant impact on our well-being. Grateful people have stronger immune systems, they're happier and more optimistic, they deal with adversity better, they are more generous and forgiving, and they feel less isolated in life.

How to do it

> Keep a gratitude journal and write down five things you're grateful for each week.

> Feel grateful for three things every morning before you get out of bed.

> Look for the good in the bad. When you have a difficult experience or memory, think about whether there's a helpful lesson within it.

> Widen your view of the world and compare your quality of life to those living in less fortunate places.

> The next time you look in the mirror, feel grateful for your physical health. Appreciate your body and how it allows you to move, smell, see, and experience life. You might even want to focus on one aspect of your physical body that you do find pleasing, rather than noticing your flaws.

15. Develop equanimity

Equanimity is a state of feeling balanced and calm, with your mind open and free regardless of what life brings. It is the ability to be at peace during difficult times and to enjoy pleasant experiences without feeling the need to cling to them.

When we're living in a truly mindful way, we learn to accept that all experiences are impermanent. Difficult emotions will come and go, as much a part of our lives as pleasant ones.

It's important not to confuse equanimity with resignation or indifference—rather it's about "allowing" things to be as they are and not trying to take charge of what is beyond your control. Equanimity allows us to be more accepting of the small frustrations and less compelled to continually seek out more than what we've already got.

If you're thinking it's not the easiest thing in the world to achieve, you're right. But when we at least open our minds to the concept of allowing things to be as they are, we open up the possibility of a much more peaceful life.

How to cultivate equanimity

> Notice what pushes your buttons, particularly the things that are largely outside your control.

> Be curious about the way you behave with people and in circumstances that irritate you. Ask yourself, "Am I taking this personally? Are there expectations that I can let go of?"

> Try to take lessons from difficult experiences.

> Watch for the inclination to hold on to experiences that bring you pleasure. Enjoy these experiences in the moment, but also acknowledge that pleasure, like pain, comes and goes. And don't minimize your enjoyment by worrying about how you'll feel once it's over.

> Take baby steps. To begin with, make room for small discomforts, then build your tolerance so that it becomes easier to accept more significant challenges.

16. Create positive "touch points"

Sometimes an entire day can go by without us even noticing the small things that make life good. Make a conscious decision to create at least three "touch points" throughout your day when you hit the pause button and bring your attention fully into the moment.

Try these

BEFORE YOU GET OUT OF BED IN THE MORNING

Resist the urge to check your email or Instagram first thing, and instead take a minute to consider what you're looking forward to in your day. If you're like most people, you might find yourself thinking about the negative aspects first (that's the way our brains are inclined), but after doing this exercise for a week, you'll find it easier to focus on the positives.

Include even the smallest pleasures: enjoying a warm shower, savoring a coffee, eating a piece of fruit, listening to a podcast on the train, or seeing a friend after work.

AS YOU LEAVE THE HOUSE

If you're in the habit of rushing outside each morning, take a few minutes after closing the door and think about how you're setting up your day. Take a breath and, in the next five minutes, focus fully on what you're doing right now. "I'm walking to the station." "I'm strapping the kids into the car, and I'm grateful for them, even though they can be a handful at times." "I'm driving, and the traffic is busy, but I'm comfortable, and the music is playing, so I'm okay."

WHEN YOU HAVE YOUR MORNING COFFEE, HERBAL TEA, OR OTHER BREAK IN YOUR WORKDAY

Check in and ask yourself how you're negotiating your day. Are you approaching things from a state of calm, or has the "rev" level you read about in Chapter 12 (page 34) escalated? Take a moment to feel your feet on the floor and remind yourself of what's actually important.

Create positive "touch points"

WHEN YOU ARRIVE HOME AT THE END OF YOUR DAY
Meditate for ten minutes or so in order to put aside your working day and really arrive home. Acknowledge any lingering thoughts from the day. Afterward, and before you rush to organize dinner or do other tasks, you may want to pause to ask your children or partner about their day.

BEFORE GOING TO SLEEP
Those minutes before you fall asleep are often when you replay your day, and this is a common time to dwell on the less favorable events or to fret about what might happen tomorrow. Before you switch off the light, take five minutes to reflect on three things that went well during your day. You may want to write them down in a notebook so that you can revisit them in difficult times, to remind you of everything that's positive in your life.

17. Create routine

One way to live more mindfully is to structure your days to fit with your natural rhythms. As you complete certain tasks over the next few days, become aware of when you feel most inclined to pursue different activities.

When do you feel most energized? This might be the best time to engage with others, to make phone calls, or to have meetings.

When are you more inclined to engage in quiet activities? This might be the best time of day to write, think, or study.

When does your energy slump? Is there something you can do to boost it, or is this the time to take things more slowly?

What about other activities, such as exercise? Do you feel focused and motivated after you're physically active in the mornings? If you exercise in the evenings, does it help you unwind? When is the best time to . . . ?

When is the best time to . . . ?

Exercise	Think creatively
Meditate	Write
Talk to friends	Make phone calls
Problem solve	Respond to emails
Make or build with your hands	Have meetings

Play with
your kids

Clean the house

Read

Put your feet up

Study

Spend time with
your pets

Do the grocery
shopping

18. A visual reminder

Often when we step back and take a look at what will really make us happy, we realize that we've made our lives more complex than they need to be. We pursue goals that won't genuinely fulfill us in the long run. We become swept up in ideas and habits that don't necessarily fit with our personal values. We do things that look good to other people without thinking about whether they genuinely bring us peace.

As you begin your journey toward living a more mindful life, you may well discover that there are several areas where you're living mindlessly.

RATHER THAN ALLOWING YOURSELF TO FEEL DISCOURAGED OR OVERWHELMED, BEGIN WITH NO MORE THAN A HANDFUL OF CHANGES.

Look back at the quiz in Chapter 2 (page 6) and choose the areas of your life where you scored a "no" or a "maybe." Create a "Living Mindfully Map" that you can look at each morning to remind you of your top priorities. Ideally, include no more than five or six areas to focus on. This will help give you traction, which is enormously beneficial in times of uncertainty.

Work at creating new habits on a daily basis and resist the urge to overhaul *all* of your life in a single week. Take it slowly to give yourself time to integrate change. Once you've created a couple of new habits, update your visual reminder, and continue to review it every few months.

Remember that being mindful isn't about being perfect, and it's not about feeling pressured or rushed to get to your goals. You'll do better some days than others. When you haven't done well, try again tomorrow.

DRINK WATER

MEDITATE
FIVE MINUTES
EACH DAY

Living
Mindfully
Map

STAY CALM

ONE THING
AT A TIME

NO GOSSIP OR
COMPLAINING

19. Use positive language

Speaking negatively, whether it's complaining about life or gossiping about others, is a drain on your energy and the energy of the people around you. It contradicts living mindfully because it stems from making judgments, and often those judgments and our frequent complaining become habitual.

It can start off as a laugh, and it can even become a way of connecting with certain friends, but keep an eye out for when negative talk begins to become your default conversation.

Start to notice yourself when you're moaning or being negative. Who do you complain to most? What are the issues you typically complain about? Most people choose a handful of topics that frustrate them and rehash these over and over again.

Use positive language

Try these

Once you're clear about your most frequent "bugbears," ask yourself whether you're complaining to the right person. Can they do something to help? If not, take meaningful action. Write a letter if it's a public issue. If the issue is a personal one, speak to the person who is upsetting you. Ask for something to be changed.

Look for what's good in the world, and take the time to share positive stories and thoughts.

Train yourself to be less judgmental. If someone thinks differently than you, ask them to tell you more about their beliefs so that maybe you can understand their perspective better.

Where possible, avoid spending too much time with the people or in the circumstances that frustrate you most. Instead, proactively seek out those who you find uplifting.

Learn to make peace with the fact that there are some things in life that you won't be able to change.

---

20. Get into the real world

In 2014, a Nielsen study found that 82 percent of Australians spend an average of 23.3 hours online each week—up from a 2003 study where 73 percent spent an average of 6.7 hours online. That's almost a whole day of every week that we're not outside walking or hanging out with friends (without our devices). And we're probably not pursuing creative activities that are better for our long-term well-being.

Make an honest assessment of how much time you spend online. Include the time you spend watching, listening to, or reading news stories on television, radio, and newspapers.

Watch for the warning signs

> Are you sleeping with your phone beside you to stay constantly connected to the world?

> Are you looking at social media when you first wake up?

> Are you posting on social media and checking for "likes" five minutes later?

> Are you binging on television episodes without taking breaks to do other things?

> Do you constantly feel the need to multitask with a device at hand?

Set up a digital detox

> Turn off all devices at a set time each day (say, from 7:30 p.m. to 8:30 a.m.) and have one day each week without access to anything online that does not help you stay mindful.

> Keep your phone on silent or in your bag when you're driving or spending time with friends.

> Get offline at least an hour before bedtime. Looking at screens reduces melatonin and can affect sleep quality.

> Don't have devices in your bedroom unless you need a meditation app or something to help you sleep.

> Stay offline at mealtimes.

> As much as possible, avoid being distracted by technology when you're spending quality time with your partner, friends, or children.

21. Appreciate beauty

Appreciating beauty and experiencing the world through each of your senses can open your heart and enhance your life in myriad ways.

Try these

SEEK OUT THE BEAUTY IN THE NATURAL WORLD
Whenever you're outdoors, be thankful for the color of the evening sky, savor the fragrance of a flower in bloom, or take a moment to close your eyes and listen to the sounds of nature.

DISCOVER BEAUTY IN PEOPLE WHEREVER YOU GO
Notice it in someone's character, hear it in the laughter of children, and appreciate it in the lines around someone's eyes (even your own if you want to be truly zen!).

LOOK FOR BEAUTY IN FINELY CRAFTED OBJECTS AND WORKS OF ART

Notice it in a painting, a carefully handcrafted item, a favorite piece of music, or a meal with quality ingredients.

ADOPT THE PHILOSOPHY OF "NONATTACHMENT"

Welcome beauty as it passes by, rather than clinging to it or feeling the need to own all of the beautiful objects you discover.

BECOME A SEEKER OF BEAUTY

Trust that there will be an endless supply of people, places, and objects that make your world aesthetically pleasing.

22. Savor food

Food is one of the greatest pleasures in life and,
when we eat mindfully, it is a source of pure joy.

Sadly, many people develop a complex and unhappy
relationship with what they eat, and they're unable to see food
as anything other than problematic. Eating mindfully is about
making your food choices pleasing and embracing a more
compassionate relationship with yourself around food.

Much of the nutritional advice we receive is confusing and
contradictory. The best way to consume is probably just to
focus on what *feels* right. Begin by acknowledging that most
foods are not your enemy—they are the nourishment that
keeps your body healthy and energized.

Instead of creating an ongoing internal struggle with what you
eat, choose foods that are pleasing and nutritious, and eat
everything that appeals to you, in the right portions.

Rick Kausman, author of *If Not Dieting, Then What?*, recommends moving away from the idea of "good" and "bad" foods, and to instead think of "everyday" and "sometimes" foods.

How to eat mindfully

> Start by finding some natural foods that you really enjoy. Make a list of them if it helps.

> Learn to determine a feeling of genuine hunger, and do your best to eat only when you're hungry.

> Watch for a tendency toward emotional eating. Don't beat yourself up when this is the case, but instead be aware of the emotions that are present, and be compassionate with yourself. You may find other tools included in this book that encourage you to manage your feelings more effectively.

> Sit down to eat every meal and don't multitask while you eat: don't read, watch TV, or browse the internet; pay attention to the experience of eating, and savor the flavor of your food.

> Eat slowly so that your body has time to register food. Put your cutlery down between mouthfuls and chew your food well.

Savor food

> Eat until you're only 70 percent full: it takes twenty minutes for your brain and body to register fullness.

> Tune in one hour after eating and see how different foods make you feel. Are you more energized or more lethargic? Start to notice the foods that make you feel good and those that don't. (For example, a fast food option might seem like a convenient lunch, but it also might make you feel sluggish and unproductive in the afternoon. Be aware of how different foods make you feel and reassess how convenient they are after all.) Trust that your body can teach you more than any article.

> Drink plenty of water.

> Where possible, eat food that is close to its natural source at every meal. Increase your vegetable and whole grain intake, and cut down on processed foods and sugar (but try not to be obsessive about it).

> Eat high-quality foods, rather than high quantity. Buy the best quality seasonal produce you can afford and taste the difference.

23. Mindful movement

Like eating, movement (or the lack of it) can be a source of guilt for many people. Mindful movement is about increasing your activity in any way that appeals to you, and tuning in to your body as you move. It's not about joining the gym or taking up running just because you should, *but instead finding enjoyable and incidental ways to increase your physical activity that strengthen and support your body.*

Moving mindfully also means being aware of when you're putting too much strain on yourself. Our bodies are designed to last us a lifetime, and we need to treat them with care. This means balancing energetic movement with stretching and strengthening, as well as discovering forms of exercise that bring us joy.

Mindful movement

Find ways of moving that you can integrate into your day

> If you take public transportation, get off a stop earlier. If you drive, park a little farther away.

> If you work indoors, get outside and walk for at least fifteen minutes each day.

> Stand up for at least three minutes every hour or so. If possible, move to a standing desk for part of the day.

> Get out of bed fifteen minutes early and do a short yoga or Tai Chi routine (you'll find lots of videos online).

> Go hiking—walk in nature.

> Do twenty squats after you brush your teeth.

> Get out into your garden on the weekend or, if you live in an apartment, join a community garden.

> Monitor your posture when you're sitting at your desk.

> Try paddleboarding.

> Join a dance class or, better still, dance to a couple of your favorite songs at home every day.

> Use the stairs.

> Ride your bike.

> Have walking meetings.

> Use a pedometer.

> Be grateful every day for the physical capabilities of your body.

24. A mindful approach to sleep

We all know that sleep is imperative for good physical and mental health. While it's important to take steps to ensure you're getting all the rest you need, it's equally important not to become obsessed with it.

Most of us will experience a few sleepless nights along the way, and sleep habits usually return to normal once outside stressors have passed. But for some people, disrupted sleep becomes a long-term problem.

One of the greatest causes of sleeplessness is trying desperately to fall asleep or stressing about being awake. Both force the body into wakefulness.

In a recent sleep research study in the United States, participants were introduced to six weeks of mindfulness training in combination with habits and practices that support sleeping well. Researchers found that the people practicing mindfulness slept better than those in a group using the standard sleep program. The mindfulness group also had a reduction in depression and fatigue symptoms.

If you're having difficulty sleeping, try the following tips, and consider taking a course in mindfulness meditation.

If you're having trouble sleeping

> Reduce naps and after waking, avoid staying in bed trying to get more sleep.

> Recognize sleepiness and go to bed as soon as you become aware of feeling tired.

> Get out of bed if you've been unable to sleep for a period of time. Give yourself an hour or so to be up, and wait for the next wave of tiredness to hit before heading back to bed.

A mindful approach to sleep

> Set reduced hours for sleeping (midnight to 6 a.m.) until your sleep habits return to normal.

> Wake at the same time every day.

> Stop screen time a couple of hours before bed.

> If you struggle to go to sleep or you're awake during the night, focus on how peaceful it is to be lying in a comfortable bed, and acknowledge that rest is valuable in and of itself.

> Listen to a guided meditation before going to sleep, and if you wake during the night, listen again to help you stay calm.

> Remind yourself that you can function well with little sleep, rather than stressing about how you won't cope the following day.

> Try not to escalate sleep disturbance by feeling agitated. Tell yourself calmly that you might be awake for a while and you'll be able to cope with that.

A simple exercise to try if you're lying awake is the 4–7–8 breathing technique. It relieves stress and has been proven to assist with sleeplessness.

WHILE YOU'RE AWAKE

Try the 4–7–8 breathing method to help you relax. Here's how you do it:

> Breathe in for four seconds.

> Hold your breath for seven seconds.

> Breathe out for eight seconds (this is generally longer than our normal out-breath).

> Repeat at least four times (or longer if you're still feeling agitated).

25. Know how you feel

Many people find it difficult to name how they're feeling. Most of us know what we're thinking, but we often lose touch with the underlying emotions that accompany those thoughts.

When we fully understand what we're feeling, it's easier to make peace with our emotions, and we usually find we're in a better place to ask for our needs to be met. For example, when your partner isn't meeting your need for connection, and you feel isolated or lonely, you can share your experience honestly, letting them know what you need, rather than behaving in an irritable or critical way.

Knowing how you're feeling gives you the chance to develop strategies for managing your emotions. If you're frustrated, irritable or tired, you can let the people around you know.

When you understand your own emotions, you'll also be better placed to recognize the way others are feeling, and you'll have a greater capacity for empathy.

Connect with your feelings

› Close your eyes and become aware of the parts of your body that are relaxed, and the parts that feel tense, tight, or even just uncomfortable. When you find a spot that seems unusual, explore exactly how that feels. Is it only a physical sensation, or is there an emotion that you notice as well? If you become aware of an emotion, give it a label. Do your best to be open-minded as you do this. If you're out of touch with your feelings, this might feel tricky at first, but with time, it becomes easier.

› After noticing and naming the most obvious emotion, ask yourself, "Is there anything else I'm feeling?" Emotions and feelings are complex—sometimes what we experience on the surface is a mask for what's underneath. Sometimes anger is a cover for fear. Bravado and aggression can cover up vulnerability. Loneliness and longing can be hidden underneath frustration or irritability. Jealousy can be a cover for insecurity.

Know how you feel

These are all legitimate and universal feelings, and it's helpful and empowering to recognize them for what they are and label them without judgment.

> Continue to be curious and open about your feelings. It might take time to make contact with your true emotions, and it may be something that you want to explore with the support of a psychologist.

What are you feeling right now?

Acceptance	Envy	Optimism
Anxiety	Euphoria	Peace
Bliss	Forgiveness	Pleasure
Boredom	Frustration	Pride
Compassion	Gratitude	Rage
Confusion	Grief	Regret
Contentment	Guilt	Relief
Depression	Hope	Satisfaction
Doubt	Loneliness	Shame
Embarrassment	Longing	Sympathy
Enthusiasm	Love	Worry

26. Be with your thoughts

As Rick Hanson, author of Hardwiring Happiness, *says, "The brain is like Velcro for negative experiences, but Teflon for positive ones."*

When you first start raising your awareness of your thoughts, you may find that many of those thoughts are negative. You might also discover a tendency to be hard on yourself when you're thinking negatively, which can create a bit of a downward spiral.

This is where one of the core principles of mindfulness comes in: acceptance without judgment.

Watch your thoughts from the place of a friendly observer. Be curious and open-minded about what goes on inside your mind. Be interested, but try not to judge.

Remind yourself that there's nothing wrong with having a negative thought. For now, take the opportunity to reflect on your thoughts mindfully.

It's from this place that you can ask, "Are my thoughts serving me? Are they current and relevant, or habitual and no longer true?"

The following activities will encourage you to become more aware of your thoughts.

Awareness exercises to try this week

> When you first wake, spend a few minutes focusing on your thoughts. Be open and curious about what goes on in your mind. This practice will also lead you to become aware of your thoughts throughout the day.

> Make a note in your journal of any repetitive negative thoughts that come up. Don't try to banish them straight away: sit with them and be open to learning about them.

Be with your thoughts

> Stay with the first thought. Avoid the tendency to escalate negative thinking by adding other thoughts about how bad you are for thinking negatively at all.

> Make peace with the fact that negative thinking is a normal part of life. Rather than feeling that you need to force those thoughts away, adopt a softer approach. You might even want to use a little bit of humor to help you change your relationship with habitual negative thinking.

> Take a break from thinking. While it's useful to be curious about your thoughts, it's tiring to spend hours thinking about what you're thinking. Once you've spent some time reflecting, get out into the real world and take little action steps that move you in the direction of your values.

27. Let go of stress

Stress can have a major impact on our well-being.
It affects our quality of life, our outlook, and even our
immune system. When we take a mindful look at
what causes us to feel stressed, sometimes we discover
that habitual tension and worry are avoidable.

Next time you notice that you're stressed, ask yourself, "What am I really stressed about?" Try to be specific. You might find it helps to bullet point your top five stressors.

Ask yourself if the level of stress you're feeling in relation to those circumstances is worth it. Are you stressing over something that is critically important to you, or is it something that is being influenced by unrealistic desires or the expectations of others?

Sometimes when we start examining stress, we discover that it's not related to anything specific, but rather that we've come to interact with all of life from a base of generalized anxiety.

If you've identified a specific stressor, ask yourself, "Is there anything I can do about this right now?" If the factors are beyond your control, acknowledge that no possible good can come of worrying about it.

If you discover that you're habitually relating to life in a stressed-out way, practice the following mini stress-busting exercise every day for the next week to help reduce the cortisol and adrenaline in your system.

Feeling stressed? Try this five-minute stress-busting exercise

Find a quiet place to sit where you won't be interrupted for five minutes. Begin by closing your eyes and breathing deeply—take the breath right down into your belly and pause for a moment before slowly exhaling. Do this at least five times and imagine that every time you breathe out, you're releasing tension. Make each breath long and soothing.

Next, scan your body from the top of your head all the way down to your feet. Notice where your muscles are tight: the common places are around the eyes, in the temples and jaw, and in the neck and shoulders. Imagine that you can soften your muscle tension as you go. When you start to relax, let your body feel heavy.

Relax into your chair. Take a few more deep breaths once you've completed the body scan and tell yourself that you're feeling calm.

Now that you're feeling more relaxed, let your mind wander back to an issue that's creating stress, and imagine you can zoom out and look at the problem from a distance. Think about how it will impact you in a year's time. Think about what advice you'd give a friend who had the same issue. Think about how one of your role models would handle it.

If you have a few spare minutes at the end of the relaxation exercise, spend some time journaling about the issue. From this calm perspective, you may find that you're able to approach problems more clearly.

Get into the habit of regularly checking in to see how much tension you're holding in your body. If you become aware that you're habitually feeling stressed, you may need to increase your exercise, meditate, practice yoga, or make time to do any of the activities that make you feel good and grounded. If you feel yourself virtually paralyzed by anxiety, in a situation you just can't handle, get the support of a psychologist who specializes in stress management.

28. Accept others

When we're too quick to make judgments of others, we create barriers in our relationships, and we don't give ourselves the chance to really connect.

Most people intend to be decent, but sometimes their actions don't meet our expectations. If their behavior doesn't fit with our view of what's "right," our inclination is to make them "wrong."

This happens often in long-term relationships; it breaks down connection and causes resentment—and, ultimately, pain. Commonly it's the very things we love about a person that causes us to feel frustrated with them in the long run. You might have loved how relaxed and easygoing your partner was when you met, but years down the track, you perceive them as lazy. Or maybe you were attracted to how structured and organized they were, and now you see them as uptight.

We need to remember that everyone has their own idiosyncrasies (and insecurities). Each of us is unique, and none of us is better or worse than another person.

If we remember this, it helps us to be more empathetic and less inclined to judge.

In the moments when you do find it difficult to accept others, start by being aware of it happening. Watch for signs that you're putting up walls, and acknowledge when you're feeling defensive or judgmental. Say to yourself, "I'm judging" or, "I want to be right." Then take a couple of breaths to give yourself time to think about how you can remain open.

It often helps us to be more accepting when we genuinely try to put ourselves in the other person's shoes. If someone behaves in a way that differs from what you believe to be appropriate, make a request for change (not in an attacking or accusing way). Do your best to stay curious and open-minded.

In the end, you may find that you can simply acknowledge your differences and accept some flaws in the other person, just as it's likely that they'll be accepting some perceived flaws in you. You may need to agree to disagree on some things, and maybe you'll need to accept that they probably won't change. When you are able to do that from a place of openness and mutual respect, it's the most liberating feeling in the world.

29. Be with positive people

When we're living mindfully, we're doing our best not to judge others. But sometimes it's also important to acknowledge how draining it can be to spend time with people who constantly see the world through a negative lens.

The principles of mindfulness include awareness, acceptance, and compassion. You can live this way and still set boundaries, which are imperative for your own well-being.

IF THE BALANCE OF NEGATIVE
PEOPLE IN YOUR LIFE OUTWEIGHS
THE POSITIVE, PROACTIVELY SEEK
OUT PEOPLE WHO BOLSTER YOU,
BUT EQUALLY, TRY NOT TO
CLOSE YOUR HEART TO THOSE
WHO ARE STRUGGLING.

When the people you're with are negative

> If you have a challenging relationship at work, find a mentor who can help you navigate your way through some of the issues.

> If you find yourself regularly engaging in negative conversation with a friend, ask them if everything is okay and listen with an open heart. Don't feel the need to resolve their issues for them.

> If a partner or family member is difficult company, try to understand what's going on for them. It may help to take a collaborative perspective and ask, "How can I help you resolve this?"

> If you know in your heart that a relationship is genuinely unhealthy, consider if it's time to move on.

Look for friends who share your interests and values. If your friendship circle is limited, attend a meet-up, take up a new hobby, or create your own interest group. Positive people feed your energy and keep you focused on the good things in life.

30. Cultivate compassion for yourself

Pema Chödrön is a Buddhist teacher who writes about cultivating compassion. In her book Taking the Leap: Freeing Ourselves from Old Habits and Fears, *she suggests that before we can be truly compassionate with others, we need to begin by being compassionate with ourselves.*

Practicing self-compassion means taking the time to get to know yourself well, accepting yourself and your imperfections, trusting yourself enough to be able to stay with difficult feelings when they arise, and extending the same sense of warmth to yourself as you would to a good friend who is struggling.

We all know that some pain in life is inevitable. When we're living mindfully and practicing self-compassion, we learn to not struggle against that pain. We become more accepting of all the experiences we encounter, and we learn to make contact with what we are experiencing and allow it to be as it is.

Be compassionate with yourself

> Notice where you're feeling most "stuck." You might find that closing your eyes helps you to make contact with your feelings. Allow your breathing to be deep and relaxed, and resist the urge to push difficult feelings away.

> Take a balanced approach to your experience. As well as not pushing your feelings away, don't exaggerate them. Don't suppress or deny them, but rather allow the emotions to be as they are. Loosen the tension around those feelings so that you cultivate a feeling of warmth and openness toward yourself.

> Offer yourself understanding and kindness. Try placing a hand on your heart as you say to yourself, "I'm okay; I can be with this." Extend kindness toward yourself.

Cultivate compassion for yourself

> Recognize that each of us is imperfect, and remember not to exaggerate your flaws. All humans suffer: it's part of our shared experience.

> Understand that we are all deserving of compassion.

RECOGNIZE THAT IMPERFECTION IS NORMAL AND WE NEED TO BE GENTLE WITH OURSELVES, NOT ANGRY OR FRUSTRATED WHEN WE DON'T MEET OUR OWN EXPECTATIONS.

31. Cultivate compassion for others

Compassion is about observing the experiences of others from your own perspective and having a desire to help. You don't need to know why someone is suffering; you simply acknowledge it and want to help alleviate it if you can.

If we teach ourselves to look beyond our differences, we begin to see the gifts in every individual, and perhaps even become aware of how we can learn from different people.

Research tells us that practicing compassion has many benefits for our physical and mental well-being. It helps to speed up recovery from disease, it can lengthen our lifespan, and it lights up pleasure centers in our brains.

Cultivate compassion for others

Maybe more importantly, it helps us to feel more connected to the people around us and it gives us a sense that we're all on the journey together.

How to increase your compassion

> Remember to cultivate compassion for yourself first.

> Assume the best in others.

> Communicate from the heart, and be willing to stay in communication rather than retreating when relationships become difficult (if you mindfully decide that the relationship is one worth maintaining).

> Recognize that you can be compassionate toward people, even when you don't agree with the way they've behaved.

> Remind yourself that everyone is doing the best that they can, with the knowledge that they have at this point in their lives.

Being compassionate doesn't mean we have to take on the role of rescuing everyone. Sometimes we have to accept that we can't help and that we shouldn't put too much pressure on ourselves to try to help. Instead, wish that person well and do your best not to judge them.

32. Forgive

When you've been hurt by someone you love or trust, it can feel difficult to forgive. But if you harbor resentment or carry a grudge, you're expending your own emotional energy and compounding the original hurt.

Forgiving is something we can all learn to do mindfully. As with all mindfulness practices, it involves letting go of judgment and accepting that we all make mistakes. It doesn't mean condoning bad behavior or accepting being treated poorly, but rather making a decision to unburden yourself of a grievance.

You may still experience negative emotions when you think about what occurred. You may not want to tell the other person you've forgiven them, and you might not want to reconcile.

If someone offends you or is hurtful or unkind, it might be a good idea to do a sanity check with a trusted friend. Articulating a grievance can let you see the bigger picture and possibly your own role in creating it. Don't consult with someone who will just take your side whatever the circumstances. Instead, satisfy yourself with the fact that this is not a situation you created yourself, isolate it, and then choose to forgive and not be affected by it anymore.

Forgiveness can sometimes still mean moving away, but importantly it is doing that without holding on to negative energy.

What is forgiveness?

> You make a decision to move on from a past hurt, and you don't let it define you or the way that you think of others.

> You value your own sense of emotional freedom: forgiving is not about the other person, it's about you.

> It allows you to live in the present, instead of continuing to rehash the past.

> Forgiveness means accepting people's differences.

> It's about forgiving yourself too.

How to forgive

> Start by writing your feelings down. Get clear about the real issues or concerns. Try to understand why things happened as they did.

> Think back to when you've made mistakes and remember how others have forgiven you, and how grateful you were for their forgiveness.

> Give yourself time to forgive.

> Remember that finding inner peace is your primary objective—revenge, negative thoughts, and wishing others harm will do little good for your own body and mind.

> Learn from past hurts. You may need to set stronger boundaries, take better care of yourself, or move away from your role as a victim.

> Practice gratitude for all of the things that are going well in your life.

33. Learn to listen

One of the easiest ways to improve your relationships is to listen mindfully. Start to really pay attention when people speak to you. Watch for your tendency to start thinking about your response (or heading toward the door) before someone has finished talking. Pay attention to what's not being said by tuning in to nonverbal cues. Sometimes body language and tone are the most effective forms of communication.

Try these tips to listen more effectively

Keep an open mind while you're listening and resist the urge to interrupt with your solutions.

Give feedback by nodding, saying "hmm," or smiling.

Encourage the speaker to keep talking by asking questions such as, "How was that?" Or offer validation by using phrases such as, "That must have been tough." Hold off giving advice unless it's asked for.

Remember, you're offering an ear, but this doesn't mean you need to find solutions to problems.

Try not to tune out, even if the speaker is boring you. Sometimes people need to tell the long version of the story to make sense of it themselves.

Do your best not to fidget, tap a pencil, turn your body away, or do things that indicate irritation or impatience.

Be the kind of listener you want others to be for you.

If you need to have a really difficult conversation and you sense that eye contact might be uncomfortable, try talking while you're walking.

34. Respond rather than react

When something unpleasant occurs, our impulse is often to react rather than to respond. Reacting is triggered by the "fight or flight" instinct, and it's generally fear-based and defensive. Responding, on the other hand, is a conscious choice. It's less emotional, more measured, and mindful.

If you're inclined to reaction, it often helps to be aware of the physical signs that generally accompany a reaction as well as your personal "trigger points."

1. PAY ATTENTION TO THE PHYSICAL SIGNS

When you feel yourself reacting, notice what happens in your body.

Tightness in your chest or stomach.

Your breathing becoming rapid.

Your heart racing.

Feeling hot or flushed.

Your muscles tensing.

Your "rev" level accelerating.

2. BE MINDFUL OF YOUR TRIGGERS

Feeling stressed.

Being ignored or not listened to.

Being tired.

Being treated badly.

Witnessing injustice or unfairness.

Feeling frightened.

Feeling irritated, resentful, or annoyed to begin with.

Feeling attacked and defensive.

3. MAKE A CHOICE

Look down the list and identify your typical ways of reacting, and next time you're feeling heated, try taking a couple of breaths and making a choice to respond.

REACTING IS	RESPONDING IS
Attacking.	Showing patience.
Getting angry.	Empathizing.
Accusing.	Asking questions.
Blaming.	Listening.
Withdrawing.	Staying present.
Avoiding.	Compromising.
Being defensive.	Cooperating.
Being overly emotional.	Staying calm.
Taking it personally.	Being rational.

35. Manage your energy

When you learn to tune in to your energy levels in a mindful way, you'll start to notice that different people, places, sounds, and experiences contribute to how energized you feel. Our energy levels go beyond how much sleep we've had, how fit we are, and what we've eaten earlier in the day (although these things do play a part too).

When life gets busy, sometimes we forget to allow time for the activities that energize us most. Often these are the same things that make us happy, so we really shouldn't treat them as optional extras.

Make time for the positive activities that you know help you feel good and centered and balanced—and watch out for the activities that drain you.

What energizes you?

Using the examples on the next two pages as a guide, make a note of the activities that inspire you and those that deplete your energy.

Exercising

Meditating

Hanging out with positive people

Spending time with kids

Getting into nature

Reading for pleasure

Doing something creative

Cooking

Playing sports for fun

Doing yoga

What drains you?

Spending too much
time online

Watching mindless
television

Comparing yourself
to other people

Consuming too many
news stories

Being around
negative people

Excessive worrying

Drinking too much

Complaining

Eating junk food

Gossiping

Overachieving

Shopping

36. Manage your time

People who live mindfully have a balanced approach to managing time. They prioritize rest, appreciate the present, and avoid getting caught up in constant striving.

They're clear about their most important priorities, and they know how to break significant goals into manageable steps so that they can stay on track without feeling overwhelmed.

The most mindful time-managers are aware of when they're procrastinating, overcommitting, or losing their focus. And they know how to bring their attention back to the most important priorities.

It helps to acknowledge that some important tasks aren't necessarily "productive" in the conventional sense.

Making time for frivolity, fun, and the activities that energize you is as important as meeting work priorities. A mindful approach is to *manage your time* instead of *letting time manage you.*

What stops you from managing your time mindfully?

> Procrastinating.

> Overcommitting.

> Having uninspiring goals.

> Not including any fun goals.

> Having no structure or routine.

> Lack of motivation.

> Reacting to every request from others immediately.

> Constantly checking devices.

> Losing focus.

Try these

Choose your priorities carefully. Review the way you spend your time, and make sure you choose activities that genuinely contribute to your happiness and well-being.

Break significant goals into manageable steps that you can schedule into a diary or calendar. For example, if your goal is to find a new role in your career, the steps might include brainstorming your ideal role, researching organizations you'd like to work for, identifying your skills and strengths, updating your résumé, setting up a LinkedIn profile, speaking to people in your chosen field, and then beginning the job search.

Take the first step and focus fully on that before moving on to the next.

Choose a difficult task that you've been putting off, and make a commitment to stick with it for fifteen minutes. Do one small thing (make a call, send an email, research more information).

If you're a habitual "over-committer," create some space in your planner and resist the temptation to fill it with meetings or other tasks. Keep some free time to give you a chance to catch up.

Turn off unnecessary alerts on social media, and allocate times when you're going to socialize online so that you're utilizing technology in a more meaningful and pleasurable way (rather than being motivated by a fear of missing out).

37. Be a role model

We might not consider ourselves role models to others as we go about our daily lives, but invariably we're modeling behaviors to the people around us—and some of these people are more impressionable than others.

Living mindfully means having a level of awareness about the kind of person you're being and doing your best to behave in ways that align with your personal values. If you think one way and act another, you're probably not behaving mindfully.

Use the following suggestions as a guide and create your own list of qualities that you want to model.

Who do you want to be?

I want to be
patient, calm, and
compassionate.

I want to be funny and
playful and not take life
too seriously.

I want to speak to
people in the way I like
to be spoken to.

I want to be a good
listener.

I want to be kind,
generous, and
supportive.

I want to treat everyone
equally.

I want to take care of
my body.

I want to be confident
and comfortable to set
boundaries.

I want to keep learning,
being curious, and open-
minded.

I want to be courageous
enough to express my
untapped creativity.

I want to be
adventurous, take risks,
and challenge myself.

I want to make a
contribution to society.

38. Take breaks

Not stopping is the opposite of being mindful. Our bodies and minds need regular breaks. Ideally, try to set aside a small amount of time every day to unwind, and at least a few hours of unplanned time every week where you can literally put your feet up and relax. There's much to be gained from regularly taking stock and reflecting on where you are at.

Read the examples on the following page and then make a note of your own preferred ways to create daily, monthly, and annual "pauses."

Try these

Block out Sunday afternoons as "commitment free" times. If you can't do this every week, aim for biweekly breaks (or monthly at the very least).

Take your annual leave, and ideally have one break each year that is at least two weeks long so that you can fully unwind. Resist the urge to make every vacation the kind where you're rushing around.

Get away from your desk to eat your lunch. Walk through the park to give you the extra boost of being in nature.

Give yourself a mental break from worry.

Take time out for an activity you love.

Book a weekend away with your partner, a friend, or by yourself.

Don't wait until you need a break—that's when taking a break will probably be a stress in itself. Plan your breaks early, so you get the benefit of them before they're urgently needed.

39. It's just passing by

The only thing we can be truly certain of in life is that our circumstances will continue to change. Each of us will experience moments of joy, love, and peace, as well as periods of suffering and grief. We will acquire and lose friends; we will have easy days and more difficult ones, and our health will sometimes give way to bouts of illness.

Many of us resist change, and we're most troubled by uncertainty. We do our best to be in control, and we like to believe that we can make plans to mitigate all of life's difficulties. You only need to look at how many insurance options we have available to us these days to understand how much we want to protect ourselves.

Being mindful reminds us that the only moment we have is the one we're experiencing right now, and in some circumstances, there's very little we can do to control what is going on around us. Sometimes the most we can do is to bring ourselves back to *this moment* and remind ourselves that for now, we only need to get through this part. That might be as much as we can manage.

WHEN YOU'RE DEALING WITH CHANGE, IT HELPS TO REMEMBER THAT NOTHING IN LIFE IS PERMANENT: EVERYTHING PASSES, AND SOMEHOW WE MANAGE TO COME BACK FROM EVEN THE MOST DEVASTATING LOSSES.

During the really difficult times, remind yourself that *this too shall pass.*

40. Connect with nature

Researchers have found that too much time spent in artificial environments can lead to exhaustion and a loss of vitality (but we hardly need research to tell us that, do we?). We just have to remind ourselves that it's very unlikely we'll ever regret going for a walk.

Those same researchers confirm that people who regularly interact with nature feel happier with their lives and have better health. Even patients in hospitals with a view of nature heal faster and require fewer painkillers than those without; people who work in offices with windows get sick less frequently, and a recent study of elderly people found that those who don't venture outside are more prone to depression.

Try these tips to reconnect with nature

Get into nature in some way at least several times each week.

Brain scans have shown that even if you can't get outside, looking at images of natural environments can lower your stress levels. Use a screensaver of a beautiful natural scene, or put a bunch of flowers or a houseplant on your desk.

Get out of the city as often as you can, even if only for a day trip. Search online for "hiking" near your local city.

Plant a garden or put some herbs in a pot.

Book your next vacation in a natural environment.

---

41. Live simply

We all accumulate material possessions that we don't really need and don't make us any happier anyway.

Buying a bigger television or a new outfit creates a momentary high that dissipates quickly, while spending money on experiences increases well-being.

Living simply means being mindful when it comes to the accumulation of material possessions: it doesn't mean going without, just not buying things for the sake of it. It's also about periodically taking stock of the objects around you and clearing space when you've created clutter.

Take some time over the next few months to go through your possessions.

How to simplify your living environment

MAKE IT BEAUTIFUL

No matter how small or unattractive your current living environment is, there are things you can do to make it more appealing. Start by tidying part of the space before considering other changes that will give it an aesthetic lift.

CLEAN OUT YOUR CUPBOARDS

Begin with one cupboard in one room. Take everything out, and before putting it back, ask yourself, "Have I used it in the past twelve months?" and, "How likely am I to use it in the next twelve months?"

Make five piles. One pile is for things you want to keep; one for things to sell; one to donate; one to throw away; and one for things you need to relocate (be careful with this pile—it should only include possessions you really need to keep but that don't fit in your existing living space).

DON'T RE-CLUTTER

Once you've tidied a space, keep it decluttered by aiming to discard one item for every new possession you bring into your home.

CREATE A SPOT FOR EVERYTHING

One of the most time-saving (and stress-reducing) practical things you can do is to give items a regular "spot" to live. If you're short on storage, consider what you need (boxes or shelving?) and take a trip to your storage supply store.

42. Mindfulness during difficult times

During tough times, our capacity to be present without judgment is usually diminished. We find it harder to sit still in meditation—yet it's at these times that we need our mindfulness practices most.

Think of these times as an opportunity to develop your capacity for equanimity and to practice self-compassion.

Remember to . . .

TAKE THINGS ONE DAY AT A TIME

Don't escalate conflict by feeling as though you need to fix everything immediately, and try not to create additional drama by scrambling around madly looking for answers.

As much as possible, experience the emotions you're aware of, allow them to be as they are, and remind yourself that you just need to get through today for now.

SAVOR SMALL PLEASURES

Remind yourself to come back to the present moment and savor the little things that make life good. Enjoy a cup of tea while sitting in the sunshine. Listen to a favorite piece of music without distraction. Treasure time spent with a good friend. These are only a few examples of the small pleasures that help us to keep perspective. Look for others that are meaningful to you.

BE KIND TO YOURSELF

Eat well, get some exercise, allow extra time to rest where possible, and try not to overcommit. During really difficult times, give yourself permission to take a "mental health day" from work (though maybe don't call it that if your boss is unenlightened!).

Mindfulness during difficult times

DON'T RUSH DECISIONS
Take your time if you need to make important calls, listen
to your intuition, and, where possible, postpone any big life
choices until after times of heightened emotion.

CONTINUE TO CULTIVATE ACCEPTANCE
Many of the challenges we face are exacerbated when we tell
ourselves we can't cope. Remind yourself that you have the
strength to deal with these challenges, and take comfort in the
knowledge that difficulties usually pass with time. Be kind to
yourself while you're drawing on your inner strength.

43. Make a contribution

Giving back doesn't mean only giving to community causes that provide you with public recognition: it also begins close to home.

Think about the people in your immediate circle who could do with a little extra help, and consider the ways you might be able to contribute. Making a contribution to others' lives gives you a helper's high, so it's often a good thing to do if you're feeling a little flat or uninspired.

How can you help?

> Offer a new parent an hour or two of babysitting.

> Drop in on an elderly neighbor who might value some company.

> Cook a meal for a busy friend.

Make a contribution

> Send a kind note to someone who needs a lift.

> Quietly carry out a random act of kindness.

> Take lunch to the homeless person you walk past every day.

> Help a friend write his or her online dating profile.

> Bring fresh fruit or a healthy snack to share with your work colleagues.

> Give a friend a hand to update their résumé.

> Help your parents set up their new computer (you'll need all of your mindfulness skills for this one!).

> Become more involved in one or two causes you're passionate about. Try to be aware of both sides of the argument, and be considerate in your communication.

> Donate or raise funds, contribute your time, write letters, or become an advocate for those in need. Put your energy into making a genuine difference with a peaceful but powerful approach.

44. Sustainable living

Each of us can make some difference to the well-being of our planet by being more mindful about how we consume and dispose of resources. When we're being defeatist we might think that our contribution doesn't matter, but if everyone made one small change it could add up to a huge benefit.

Ways to live more sustainably

> Buy less processed food.

> Stop buying bottled water.

> Reduce litter by taking your own shopping bags.

> Start a compost bin.

> Change to environmentally friendly cleaning and skincare products.

Sustainable living

> Buy foods that are in season and locally produced.

> Reduce your energy consumption. Put on an extra sweater in winter, use a fan instead of the air-conditioning, and cut back your shower time.

> Support local, ethical, and sustainably run businesses.

> Grow your own veggies or join the local community garden.

> Recycle glass, paper, and plastics.

> Fix leaky taps and install low-flow showerheads.

> Change to low-energy light globes.

> Repair items rather than throwing them away.

- Buy nothing new (other than food) for at least two months of every year.

- In summer, sleep with a sheet—not the duvet with the air-conditioning on.

- Close the blinds to keep the heat in or out.

- Change the thermostat on your heating or air-conditioning.

- Next time you buy a new appliance, choose one with the top energy rating.

- Plant a tree.

- Invest in solar panels or switch to a power company that uses renewable energy.

45. Shape your spirituality

Thich Nhat Hanh is a Zen Buddhist and an advocate for world peace. One of his key messages is that we must learn not to be fanatical about any doctrine or ideology (he even includes his preferred spiritual school of Buddhism in this message). He believes that we should explore different forms of spirituality as "tools for insight and understanding," rather than a set of messages that we need to fight over.

If you're drawn to the idea of deepening your connection with spirituality, consider exploring it on your own terms. You may find it helpful to discard labels and dogma—instead, start gathering your own ideas about what it means to live a spiritual life.

Try not to judge another person's practice as better or worse than your own. Instead, be curious and ask questions—being mindful about spirituality means staying open to new ideas.

If you're drawn to spirituality, but you're unclear about what that means for you, meditate on it and trust your intuition. You may find that meditation helps you to sense that you're making a connection with a "higher consciousness" of some kind. But keep in mind, there's no single "right way" to be spiritual. Allow yourself to be guided by your internal wisdom.

IT MAY EVENTUALLY FEEL RIGHT
TO SEEK GUIDANCE FROM OTHERS,
BUT REMIND YOURSELF THAT
YOU WILL KNOW WHEN
SOMETHING IS RIGHT FOR YOU.

Try these

Start to really listen to
your intuition.

Pay attention to everyday
experiences that you
would usually pass off
as coincidences.

Learn to tune in to the
energy of people and
places.

Try visualizing.

Meditate.

46. Develop nonattachment

One of the principal tenets of mindfulness is that it's important not to be attached to life unfolding in a certain way. Most of our suffering occurs when we want things to be different or when life doesn't go to plan. At a practical level, we know that everything will unfold as it unfolds, but it's still tempting to want to control what we can.

Nonattachment means . . .

> You're no longer ruled by the expectation that life will be rosy every day.

> You are able to let some things go. You still don't tolerate harmful behaviors, but you're able to greet life's most difficult challenges with compassion, not anger or frustration.

Develop nonattachment

› You're not cold or indifferent. Emotions still arise, but you have the capacity to give them space, and you have a greater sense of perspective.

IT'S HELPFUL TO REMEMBER
THAT EVEN DIFFICULT TIMES
OFTEN INCLUDE LESSONS THAT
ARE ESSENTIAL FOR OUR GROWTH.
YOU MAY EVEN FIND THAT DOWN
THE TRACK YOU'RE GRATEFUL FOR
AN EXPERIENCE THAT SEEMED TO BE
DEVASTATING AT THE TIME.

With a dedicated focus on cultivating a mindful attitude to life (meditation will help), you'll begin to discover that your mind becomes open and, to put it simply, more able to go with the flow.

47. Do more to do less

When you start the process of making your life less complex, sometimes you discover that, in the short term, it seems to add to your workload! Resist the urge to overhaul your entire life in a single weekend (or to toss this book to the side because it all feels too difficult).

Remind yourself that "living mindfully" is not something that can be achieved overnight. And it's not like a switch, where you're either doing it, or you're not; there are *degrees* of mindfulness, and you can be living more mindfully or less mindfully. Just reading this book means you're already living more mindfully. Life is ever-changing and uncontrollable, so despite our best efforts to create order and simplicity, we'll always be facing challenges. It's how we approach those challenges that will make the difference.

Do more to do less

Understand that creating awareness and change in some areas of your life is going to take some extra effort to begin with. But in the long run, creating more order (or, more accurately, a level of order that suits you) will alleviate pressure.

Remember to . . .

› Pace yourself. Start with baby steps.

› Be kind to yourself.

› Take it slowly.

› Make the changes you want to make without the desire to perfect your life.

› Go with the flow.

48. "Uncomplicate" your life

We're often our own worst enemies when it comes to keeping things simple, and we make life more complex than it needs to be. We respond to other people's needs more readily than taking care of our own; we say "yes" when we really mean "no," and sometimes we get swept up in other people's dramas. Much of the difficulty we perceive in life is actually just played out inside our own minds.

How to alleviate some of the complexity

1. DO WHAT'S RIGHT FOR YOU

Give up on trying to please everyone else. Listen to what your heart tells you is right. Be ethical, kind, generous, and creative, but also have the courage to say "no" every now and then.

"Uncomplicate" your life

Trust your intuition in difficult situations. Pause before responding to new requests. Take your time before finalizing big decisions and, most of all, do what's right for you. Self-care is not the same thing as being "selfish." When you look after yourself well, you'll have an abundance of energy to give to others.

2. BE HONEST

There are many ways in which we're not truthful. We don't let a manager know when we're not coping; we don't say, "I'm sorry," early enough; we don't reach out and say, "I can see that you're struggling," as often as we should.

Many complex situations can be nipped in the bud by a courageous, open conversation. Be the person who is known for authenticity. This doesn't mean telling others what is wrong with them, but rather knowing what's true for you and having the integrity to stand by it.

3. DISCONNECT FROM DRAMA

Regardless of what's going on around you, make a choice to stay centered and calm. When other people start heating up and tension rises, take a few breaths and make an active choice not to engage in drama.

Remember, you don't need to accept every invitation to argue, and you don't need to be swept up in the storm.

4. "UNDERTHINK" IT

Step away from what's worrying you and bring yourself back to the moment. Is there one small positive action step you can take now? If there's literally nothing you can do, take a few breaths and remind yourself that nothing in this world is permanent and that the only moment you really have is the one you're living in right now.

49. Turn toward discomfort

In his book The Mindful Path to Self-Compassion, *Dr. Christopher Germer outlines a simple formula that describes how we exacerbate our suffering.*

PAIN X RESISTANCE = SUFFERING. "Pain" refers to the inevitable difficulties we experience, "resistance" is the effort we make to push that pain away, and "suffering" is the end result.

Imagine that our pain is at a level of 7 (out of 10), and we resist it strongly. If we give that resistance a score of 100, it means that the suffering we feel is equal to 700. But if we resist the pain by 10 points, our suffering amounts to 70. Ultimately, if we can get our resistance to zero, our suffering also becomes zero.

Measuring pain and resistance in this way is not a scientific formula; Dr. Germer's approach is a simple reminder that *our suffering is exacerbated by how much we resist it.*

He introduces a five-step process that helps us to understand the stages we might go through to move from resistance to peace.

AVERSION. This is where we resist, avoid, or overlook uncomfortable feelings. In this stage, we do things to numb our feelings, such as overeating, shopping, gambling, drinking, or taking drugs.

CURIOSITY. If we can stay with our experience and turn toward the discomfort, we can be open and curious, and ask questions such as, "What has caused this?"

TOLERANCE. We start to endure the pain, but we still wish it would go away.

ALLOWING. We begin to let the difficult feelings come and go on their own.

FRIENDSHIP. We start to embrace everything we feel, and we see hidden value in even the difficult experiences.

Moving through these steps takes time, and it's not always a linear process. It's likely you'll take two steps forward and another one backward along the way. You may find that it helps to meditate and to remember that the first step is to just be aware of where you are in the process.

50. The middle way

One of the biggest stumbling blocks that people encounter when they attempt to live mindfully appears when they're trying to get it perfectly right.

Instead of putting yourself under pressure to achieve a perfectly mindful life, try taking what the Buddhists call "the middle way."

This is where we find a path that sits between being consumed by your difficulties and pushing them away. The middle way means not believing you must live a life of austerity in order to be a good person, but equally not getting caught up in being overly extravagant. You don't try to control everything around you, but at the same time, you don't sit around waiting for a good life to come your way.

The middle path is about being the best person you can be, cutting yourself some slack when you make a mistake, and, maybe most importantly, remembering not to take it all too seriously. Life is better when you remember to laugh—and being able to laugh at yourself is part of that.

The middle way according to Buddhist philosophy

> Have the right view of life. Know that there will be suffering and joy. Try not to push away the difficult experiences or cling to the enjoyable ones. Make room for everything.

> Have the right intention. Aim to be compassionate, to not create suffering, and to act in ways that make the world a better place.

> Try not to say things that will hurt others; be honest and avoid gossip.

> Take the right actions. Help others, live ethically, don't harm living creatures, and take care of the environment.

> Do the right kind of work. Take a job that doesn't cause harm to others and, where possible, do work that makes a meaningful contribution to the world.

> Have the right mental attitude. Encourage positive, helpful thoughts, and do your best to discourage destructive ones.

> Be mindful. Be aware of what you think, feel, and do.

> Use meditation to help you achieve a higher level of awareness.

Acknowledgments

With special thanks to the wonderful efforts of Melissa Rhodes Zahorsky and Julie Barnes for creating this beautiful edition of my second book.

Thank you also to the extended team at Andrews McMeel including Kirsty Melville, Dave Shaw, and Tamara Haus for giving me the opportunity to publish in the United States and for making the experience so seamless and enjoyable.

Thanks also to Affirm Press for helping me to fulfill my lifelong dream of becoming a published author all those years ago.

And as always, a big thank you to my family—Chris, Elsa, Meg, Toby, and Oscar—for helping me to live more in the moment and savor the small treasures that make life beautiful.

About
Kate James

Kate James is a coach,
mindfulness teacher,
speaker, and writer.

Through her business,
Total Balance, Kate helps
her clients find their
direction and build
self-belief.

She is a popular
teacher on the
free Insight Timer
meditation app
and the author of
four bestselling
books.

 @total_balance

 @totalbalancegroup

References

Chapter 7   Hedonic adaptation: http://www.sonjalyubomirsky.com/files/2012/09/Sheldon-Lyubomirsky-2012.pdf

Chapter 8   Women and anxiety: http://www.adaa.org/living-with-anxiety/women

Multitasking and productivity: http://news.stanford.edu/news/2009/august24/multitask-research-study-082409.html

Chapter 14   The benefits of gratitude: http://www.health.harvard.edu/newsletter_article/in-praise-of-gratitude

Chapter 16   The brain's inclination to focus on the negative: https://www.psychologytoday.com/blog/wired-success/201406/are-we-hardwired-be-positive-or-negative

Chapter 20   Nielsen statistics for hours spent online: http://www.nielsen.com/au/en/press-room/2013/ten-year-analysis-reveals-australias-thirst-for-connected-devices.html

Chapter 24   The 4-7-8 breathing technique: http://www.dailylife.com.au/health-and-fitness/dl-wellbeing/the-method-used-to-fall-asleep-in-just-one-minute-20150601-ghe1lp.html

Chapter 31   The health benefits of compassion: http://greatergood.berkeley.edu/article/item/compassionate_mind_healthy_body

Chapter 40   Exhaustion and loss of vitality caused by artificial environments, and the benefits of spending time in nature: http://heapro.oxfordjournals.org/content/21/1/45.full

Be Mindful and Simplify Your Life

Andrews McMeel Publishing
a division of Andrews McMeel Universal
1130 Walnut Street, Kansas City, Missouri 64106

www.andrewsmcmeel.com

20 21 22 23 24 SDB 10 9 8 7 6 5 4 3 2 1

ISBN: 978-1-5248-6220-6

Library of Congress Control Number: 2020941203

Be Mindful and Simplify Your Life was first published
in Australia in 2016 by Affirm Press.

Editor: Melissa Rhodes Zahorsky
Art Director/Designer: Julie Barnes
Production Editor: Jasmine Lim
Production Manager: Tamara Haus

ATTENTION: SCHOOLS AND BUSINESSES
Andrews McMeel books are available at quantity discounts with
bulk purchase for educational, business, or sales promotional use.
For information, please e-mail the Andrews McMeel Publishing
Special Sales Department: specialsales@amuniversal.com.